David Lanz

Joy Noel

Visit David online at **DavidLanz.com**

Joy Noel artwork by Daniela Boifava
Vision Gate Design - **visiongate.com**

Special thanks to Kathy Parsons
MainlyPiano.com

ISBN 978-1-4803-4324-5

HAL•LEONARD®
CORPORATION
7777 W. BLUEMOUND RD. P.O. BOX 13819 MILWAUKEE, WI 53213

Visit Hal Leonard Online at
www.halleonard.com

Joy Noel

After enjoying a certain amount of success as a recording artist in the late 1980's and 1990's, I knew it was inevitable Narada, my label during this time, would ask me to record a Christmas album. I had contributed to several of their holiday collections including 1985's *Solstice*, with Canadian pianist Michael Jones and I equally sharing the spotlight, but the time was drawing near for me to step out on my own.

I spent several years selecting and arranging my favorite carols, in between touring and other recording dates, and then in 1994 my first solo holiday album, *Christmas Eve*, was released. In concert I have referred to this collection of well-known carols, with my tongue firmly planted in my cheek, as "Presbyterian's Greatest Hits!"

There were big changes ahead in the late 90's as my manager, W. F. Leopold, procured a new contract for me with Decca Records. Then shortly after leaving Narada in 1999, they released *The Christmas Album*, culled from a live 1989 holiday concert at the Guthrie Theater in Minneapolis, selections from *Christmas Eve*, and several of my non-holiday songs that fit the tone and mood of this collection.

The following year I created a new solo piano recording for Decca entitled *Angel in My Stocking*; holiday music and solo renditions of several pieces from my *World at Peace Concerto*. (From the Grammy nominated *East of the Moon*.)

Angel in My Stocking was originally only available for a one-day sale on a home shopping cable channel back in 2000. This happened to be on the very same day as the long awaited announcement of the dramatic Bush/Gore presidential election results, a day most of us here in the USA were glued to our televisions, more interested in the counting of the "hanging chads" than in shopping! After this one-day sale, the recording went back on the proverbial shelf.

Then in 2004 a limited edition CD of *Angel in My Stocking*, with a few bonus tracks, was created and given a bit more distribution via my website and live performances, however, it has never been widely available.

Now, with five new solo piano holiday pieces, an arrangement of John Lennon's classic, *Happy Christmas (War is Over)*, several newly recorded and re-released carols from *Angel in My Stocking*, and a handful of snowy improvisations, I am happy to offer you this new holiday music collection.

My wish is that this music will help to create a sense of peace and celebration in your home and add a dash of the true spirit of the season.

The spirit of JOY ...the spirit of *Joy Noel*

Wishing you the best that the holidays have to offer and many New Year's blessings... from my family to yours,

David Lanz

JOY NOEL PRELUDE

By DAVID LANZ

Very freely

Pedal ad lib. throughout

HAPPY XMAS
(War Is Over)

Written by JOHN LENNON
and YOKO ONO

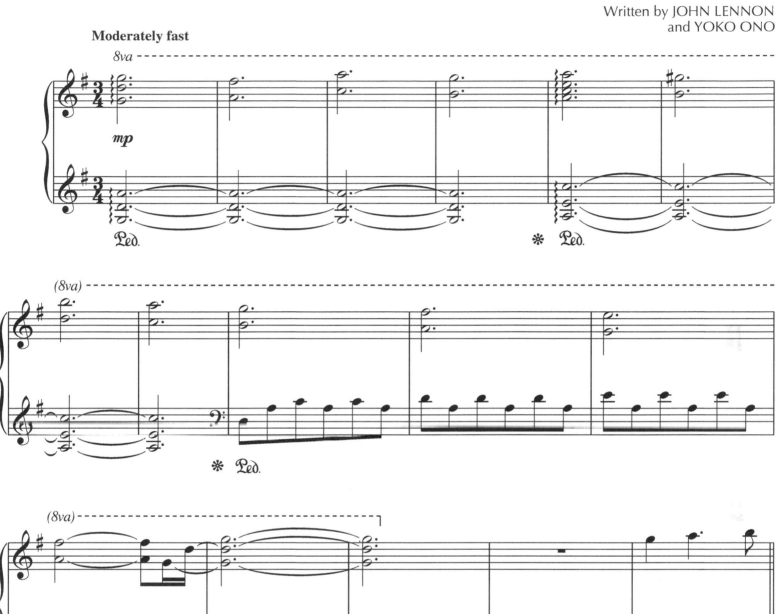

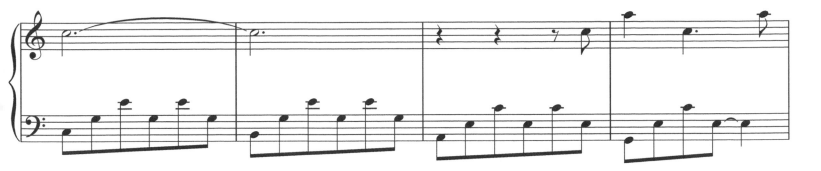

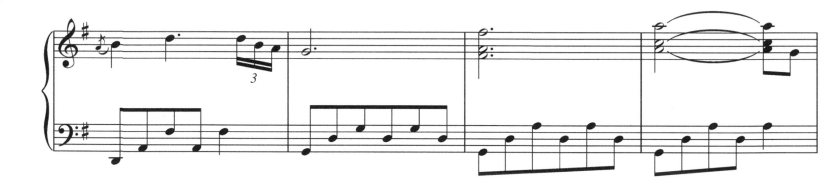

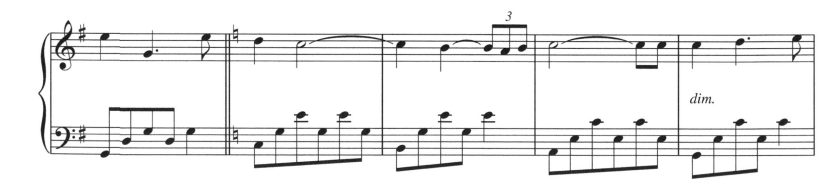

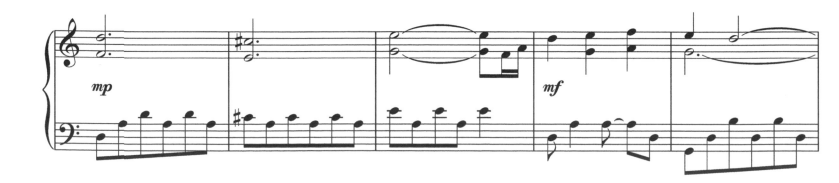

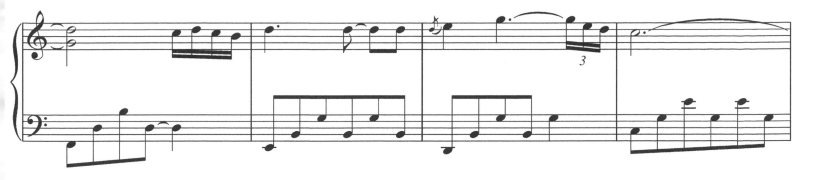

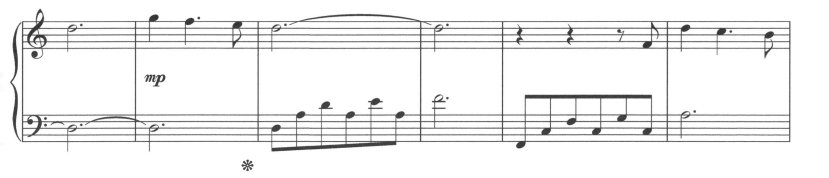

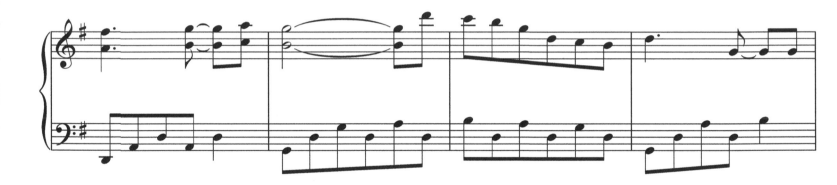

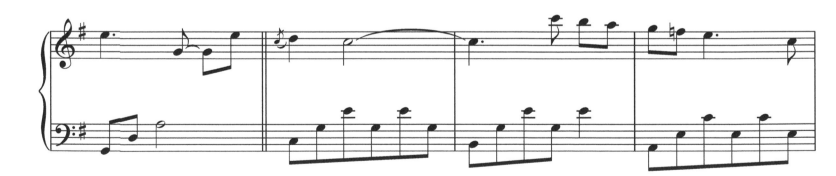

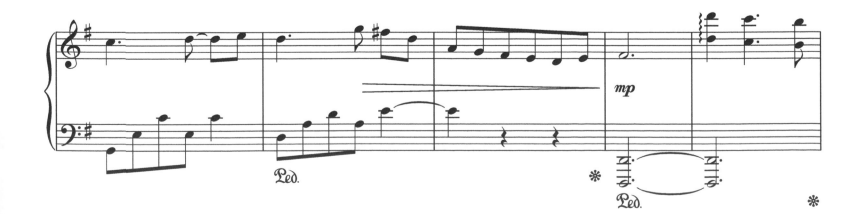

Ped.   * sim.

Gently

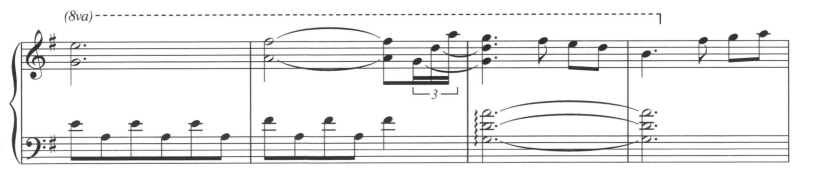

COVENTRY CAROL

Traditional
Arranged by DAVID LANZ

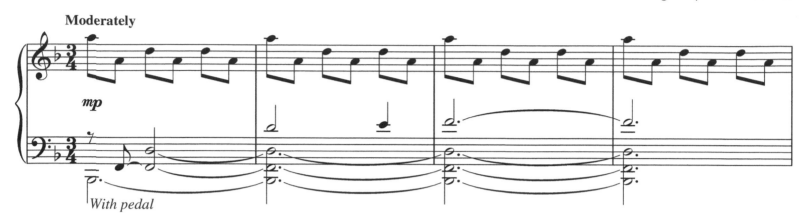

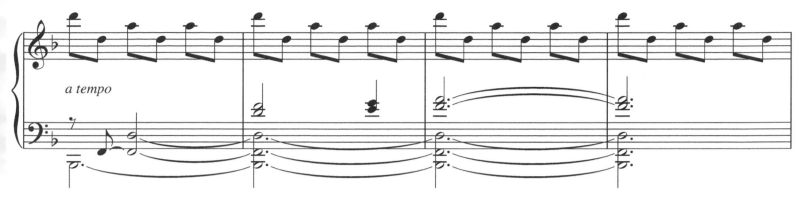

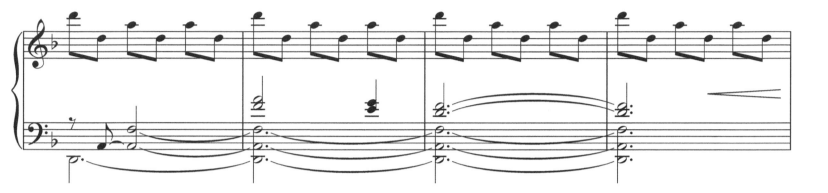

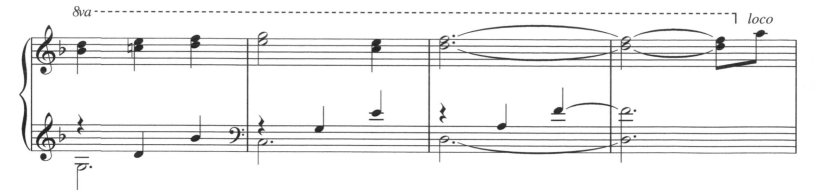

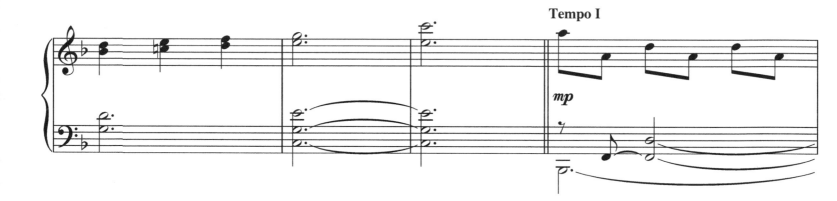

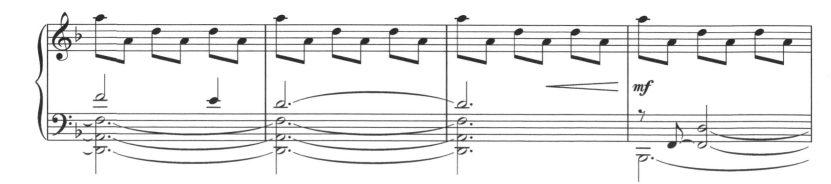

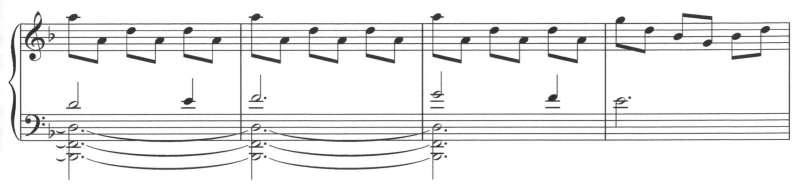

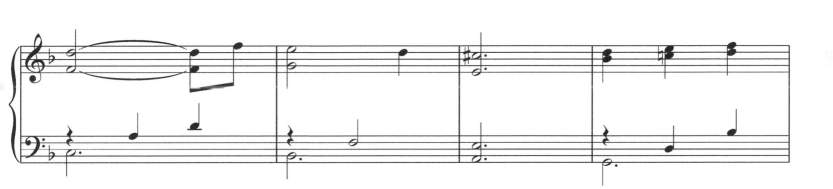

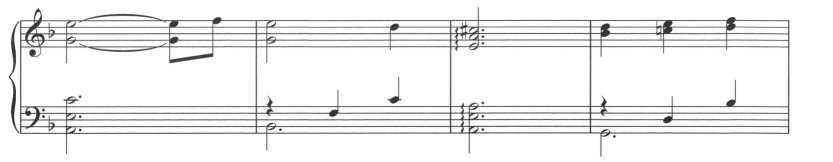

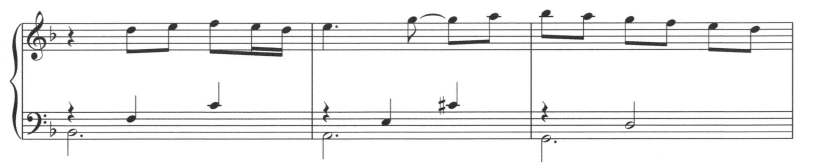

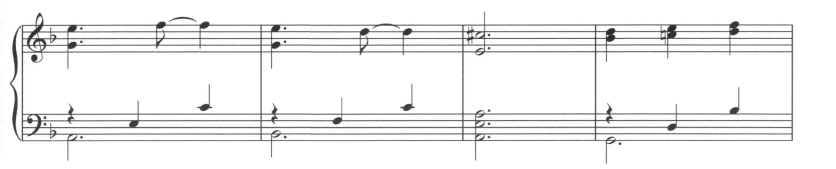

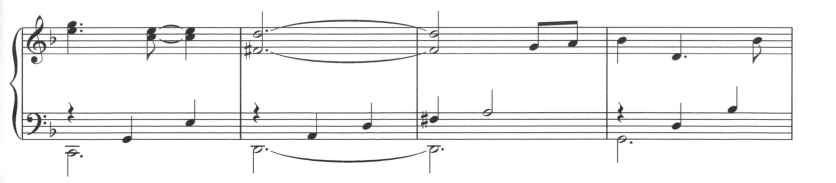

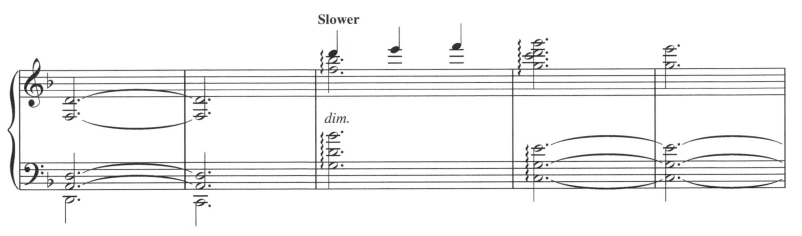

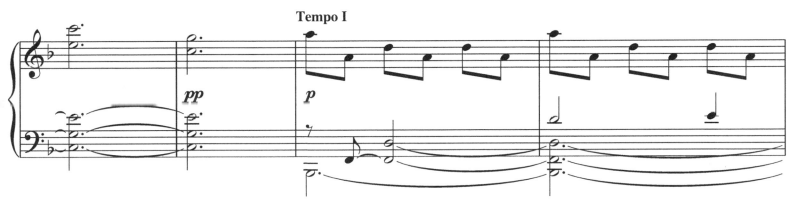

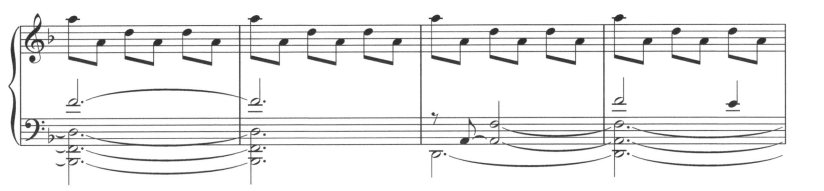

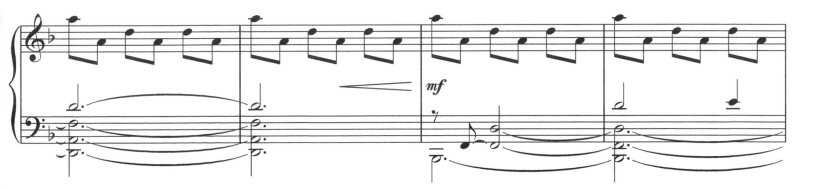

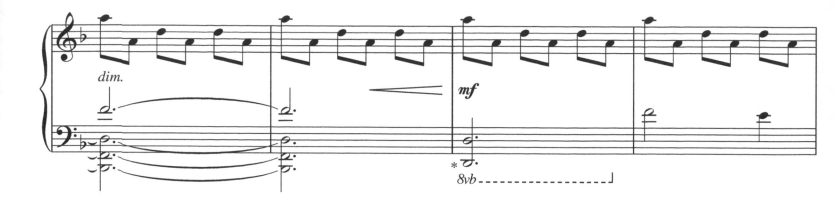

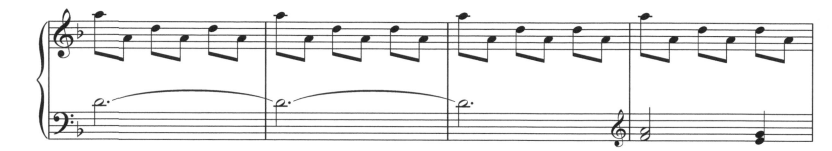

Let ring to end.

JINGLE BELLS

Traditional
Arranged by DAVID LANZ

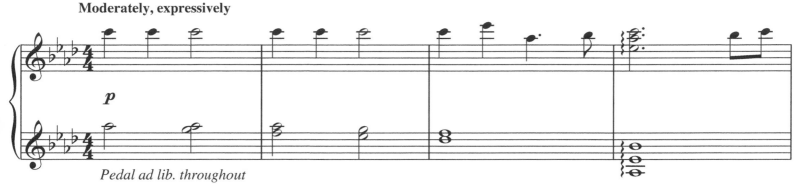

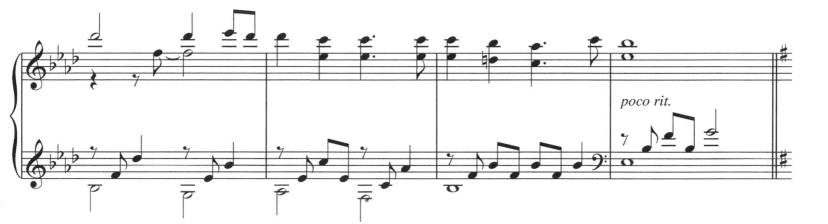

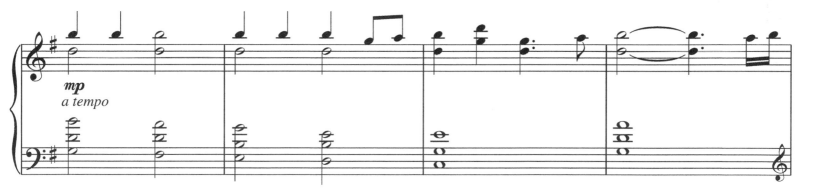

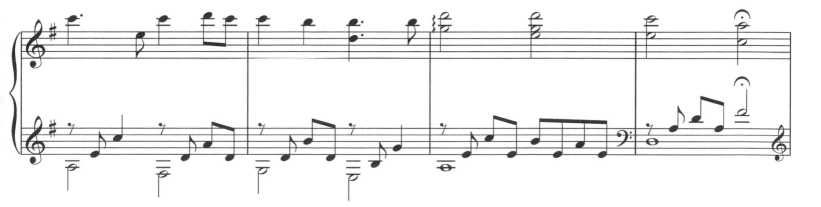

More steadily, faster

Tempo I

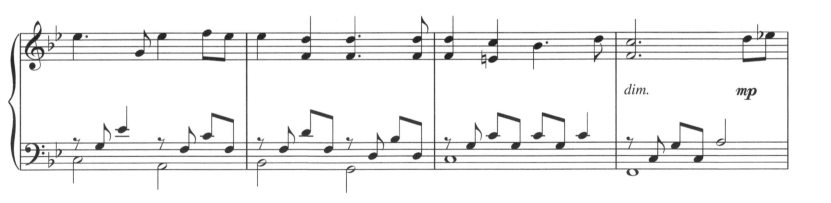

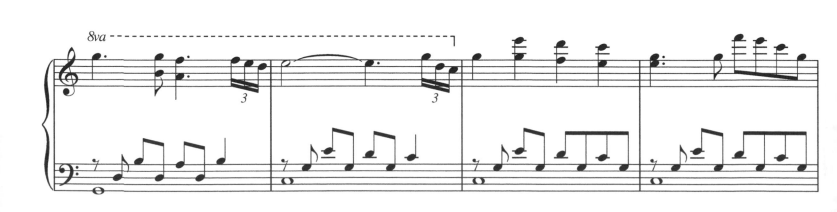

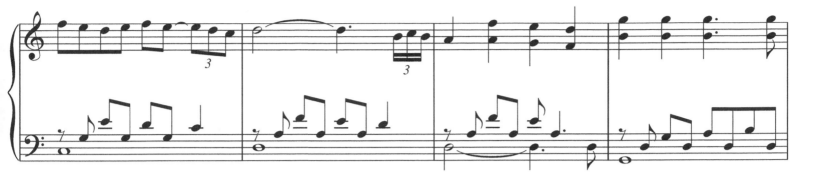

BRING A TORCH JEANETTE ISABELLA

Traditional
Arranged by DAVID LANZ

Moderately

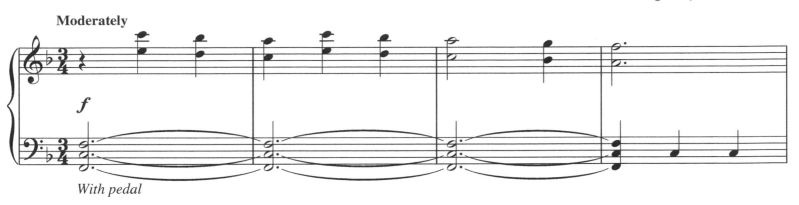

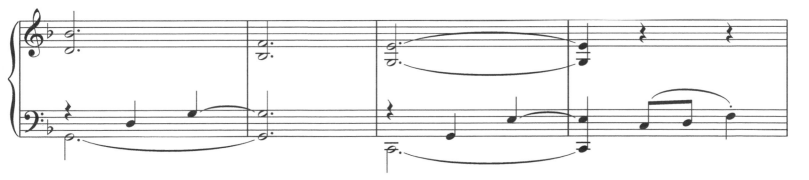

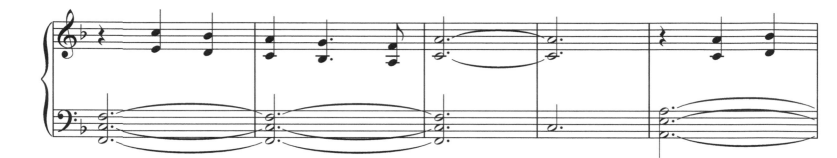

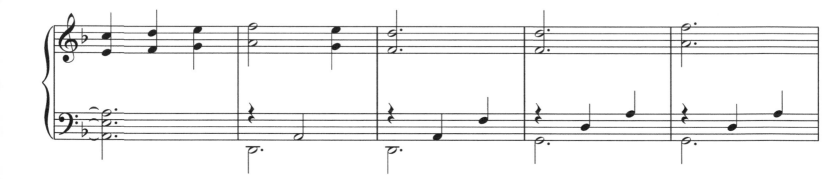

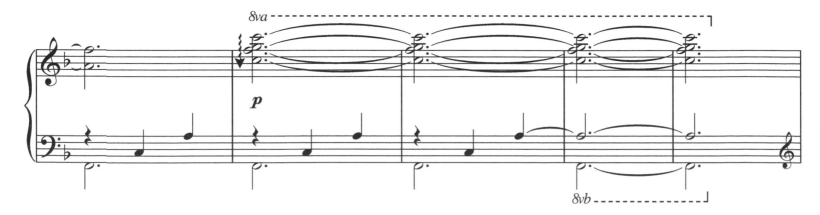

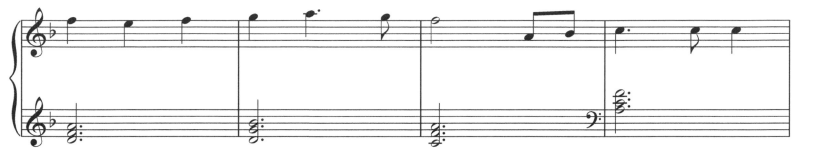

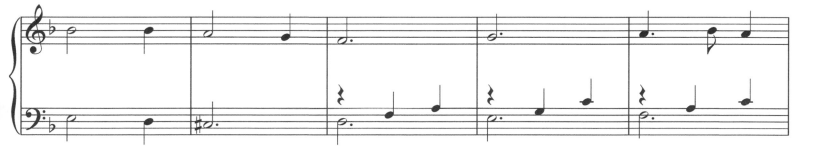

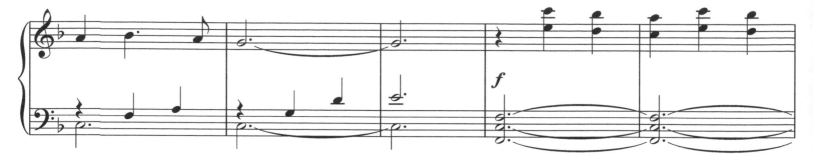

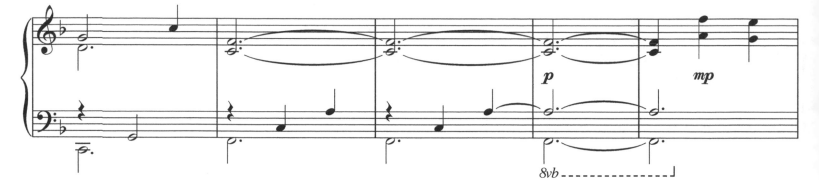

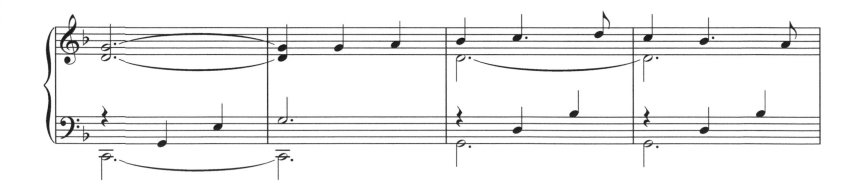

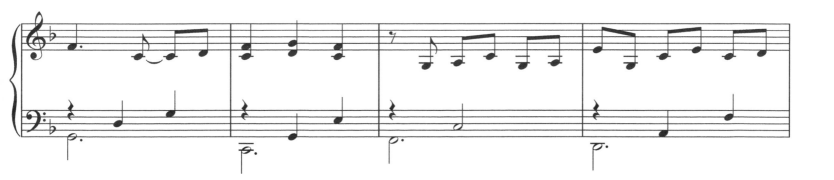

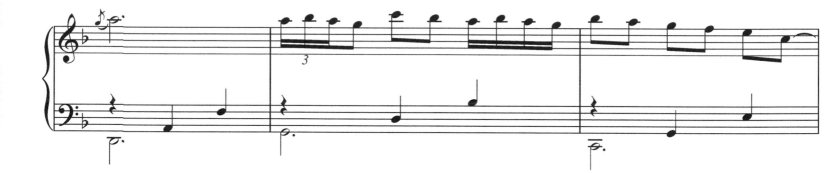

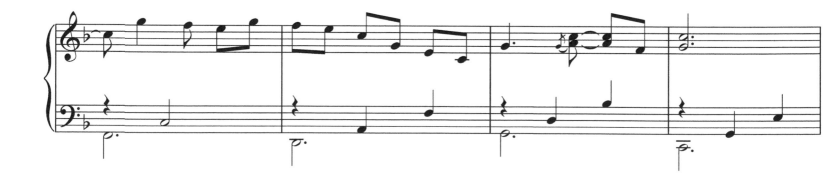

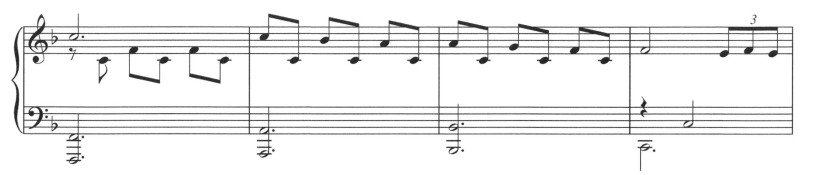

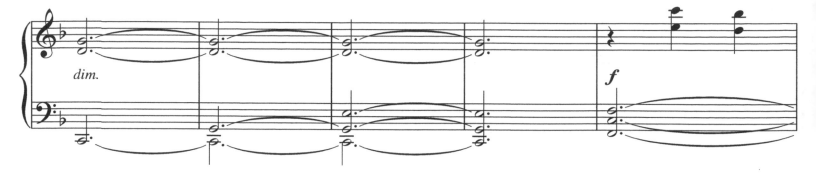

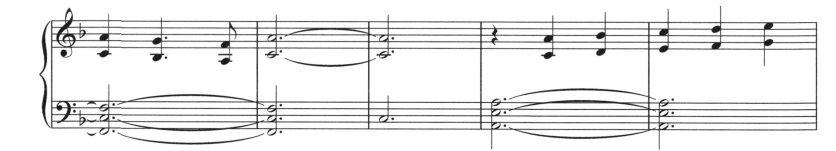

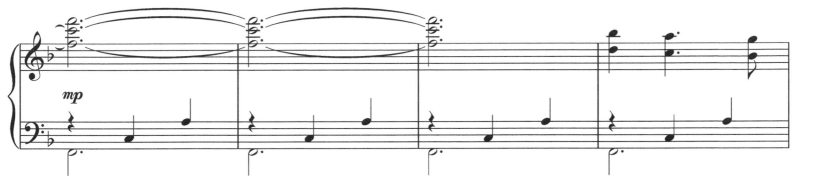

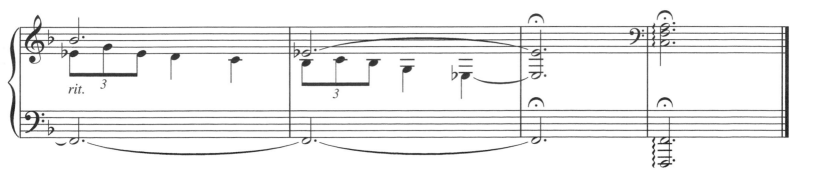

"O'ER THE FIELDS..."

By DAVID LANZ

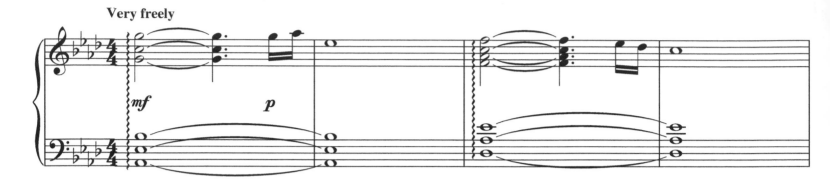

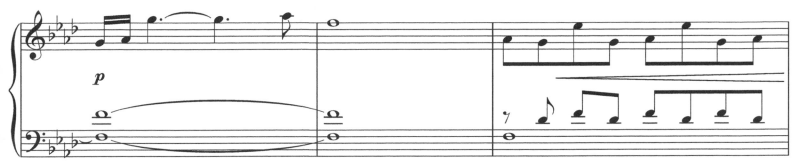

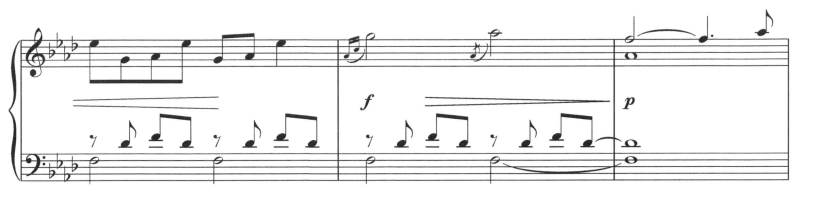

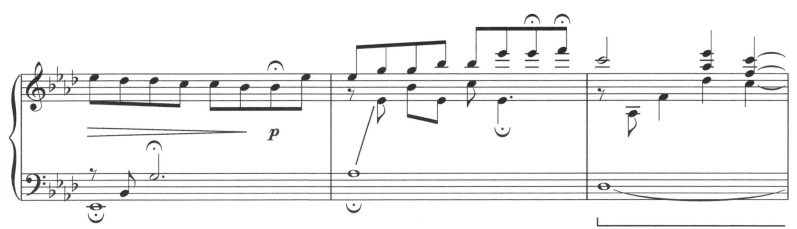

NOEL NOUVELET

Traditional
Arranged by DAVID LANZ

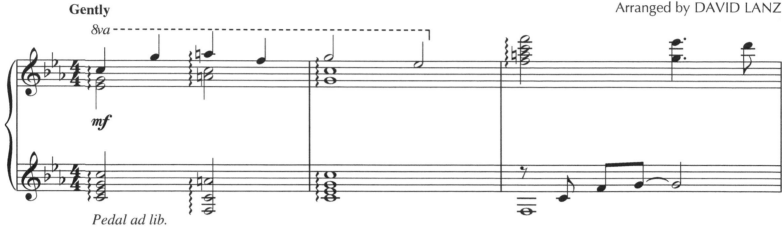

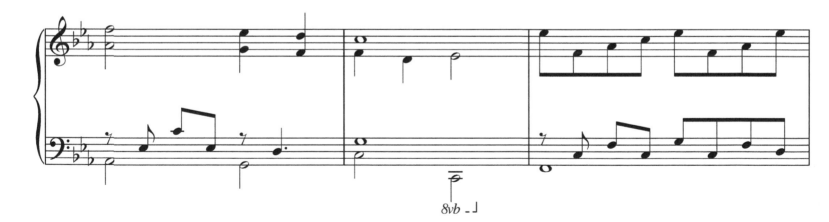

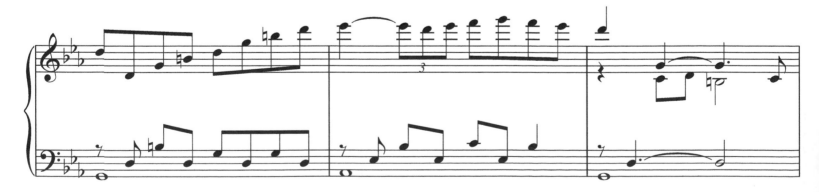

Moderately fast, in 2

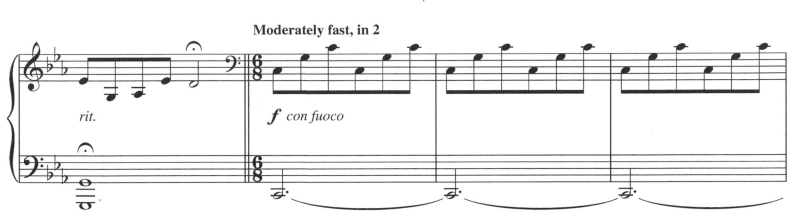

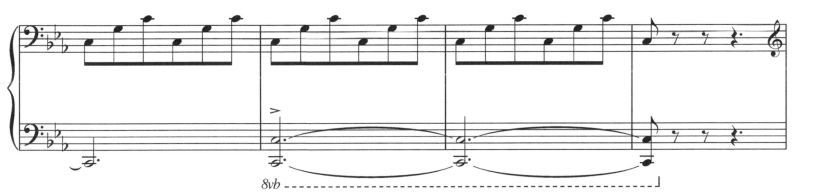

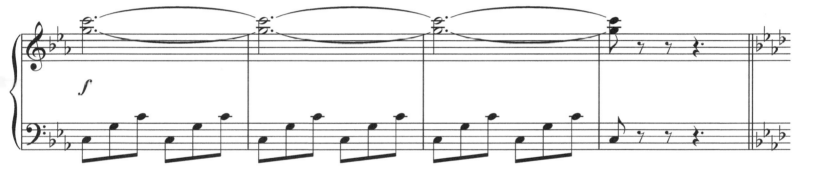

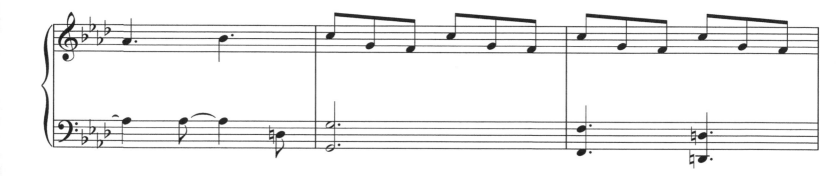

1.

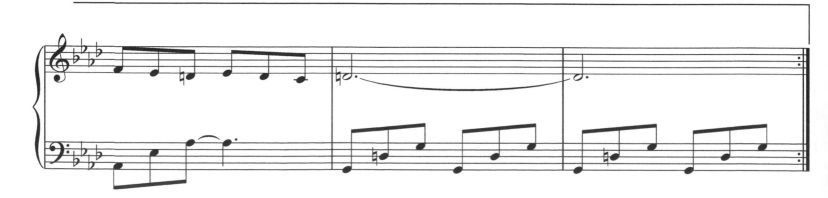

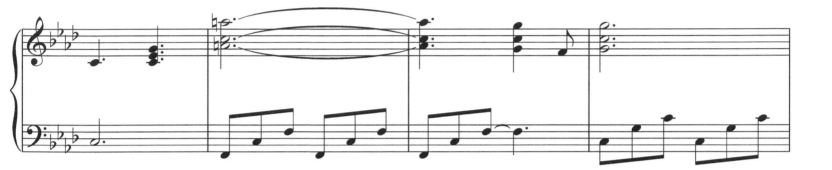

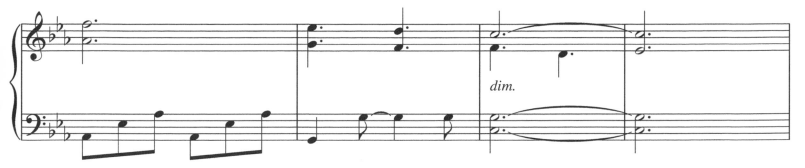

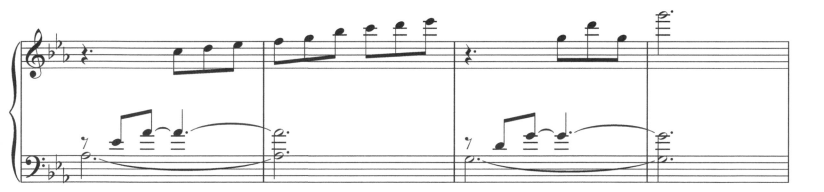

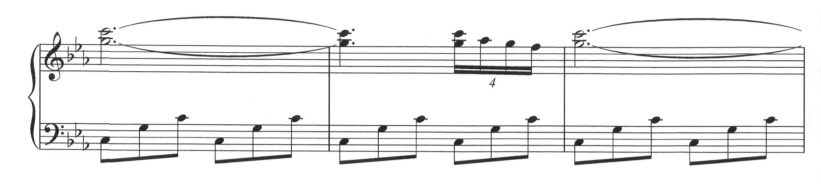

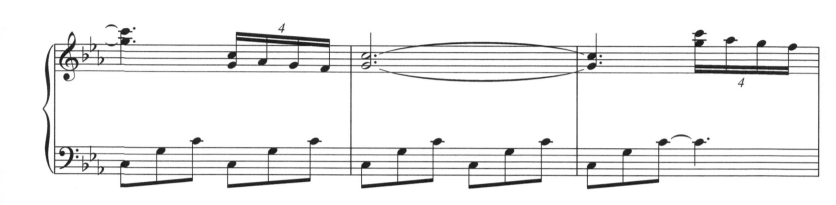

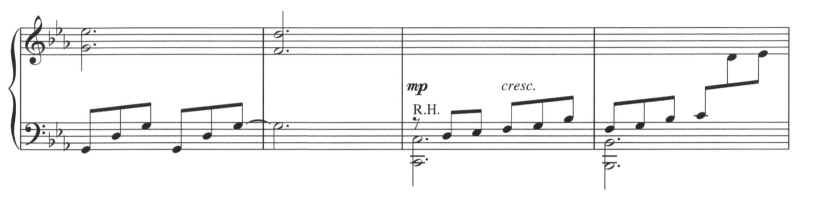

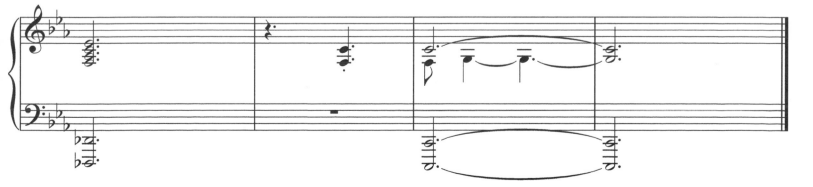

GOOD KING WENCESLAS

Traditional
Arranged by DAVID LANZ

Moderately slow

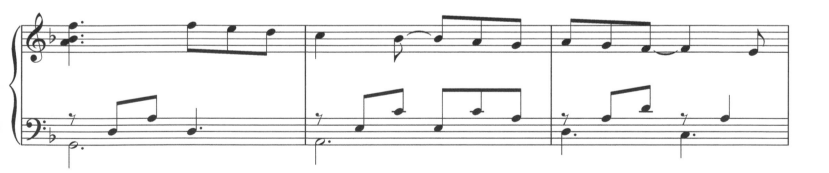

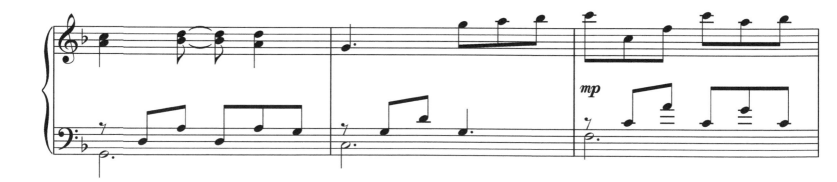

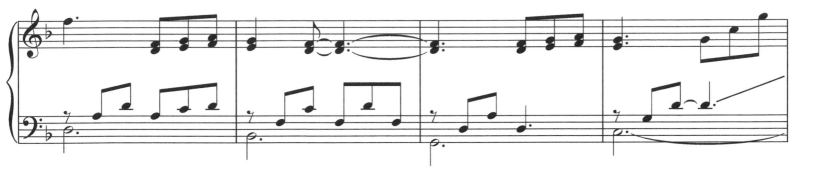

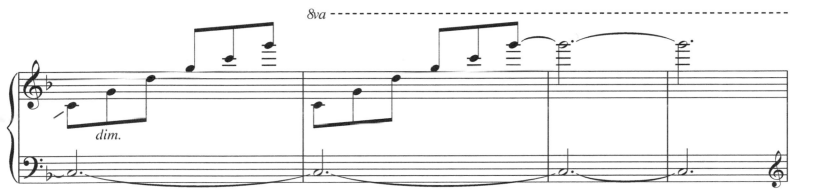

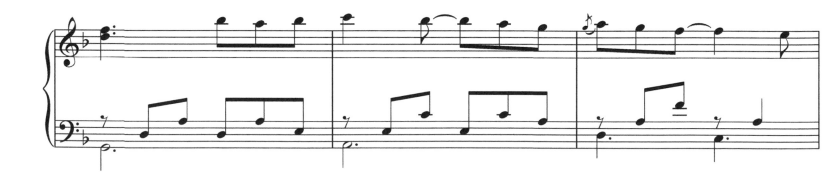

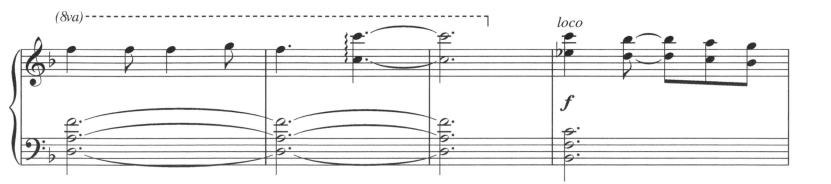

ON CHRISTMAS MORNING

By DAVID LANZ

Very freely

Pedal ad lib. throughout

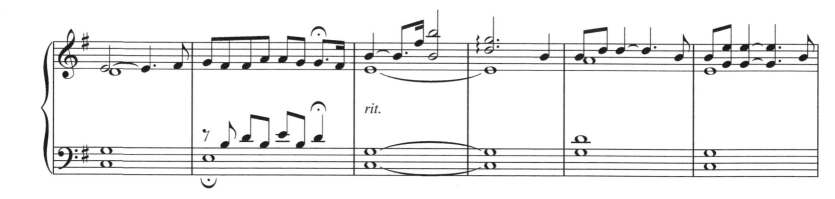

ANGEL IN MY STOCKING

By DAVID LANZ

Moderately fast, lightly

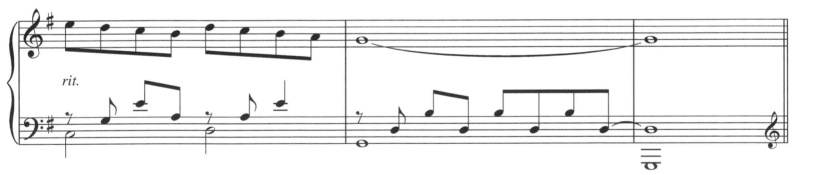

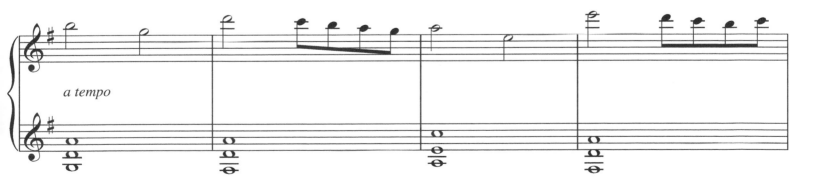

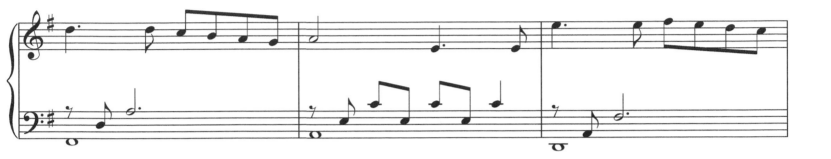

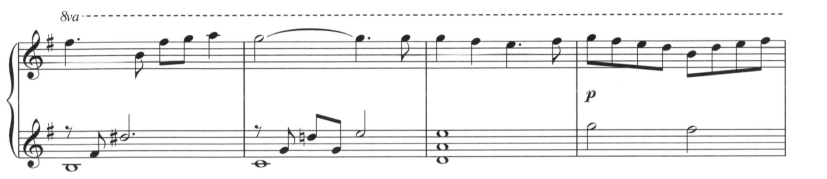

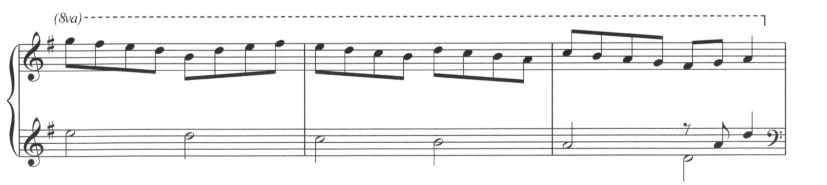

CAROL OF THE BELLS

Traditional
Arranged by DAVID LANZ

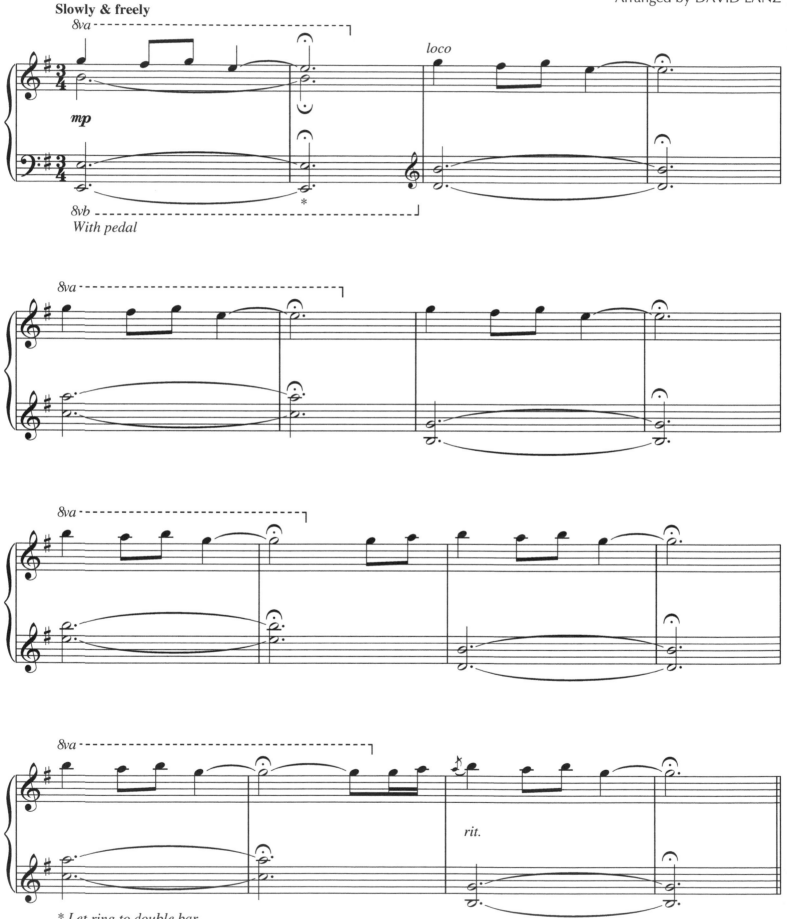

* *Let ring to double bar.*

65

Livelier

8va

mf

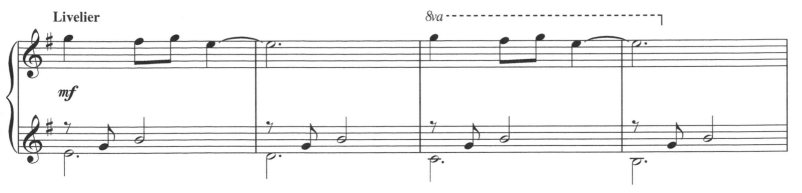

8va

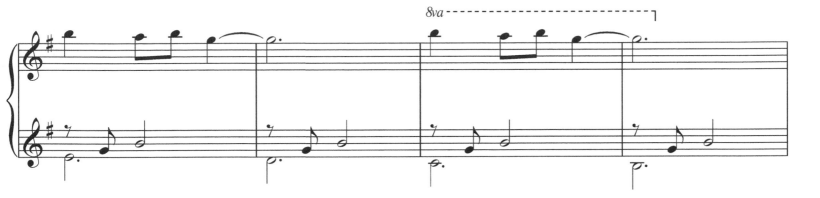

cresc.

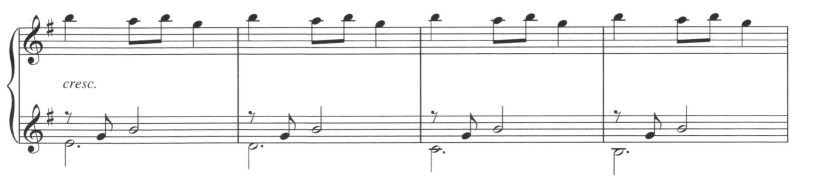

f

rit. e dim.

p

mf

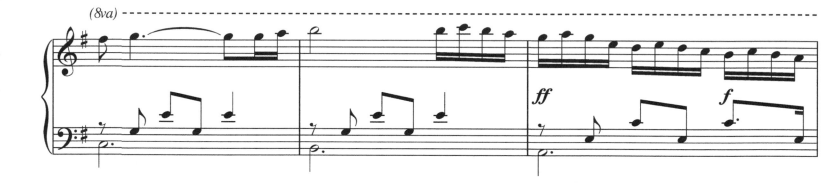

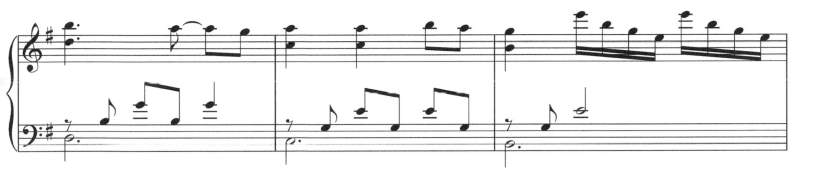

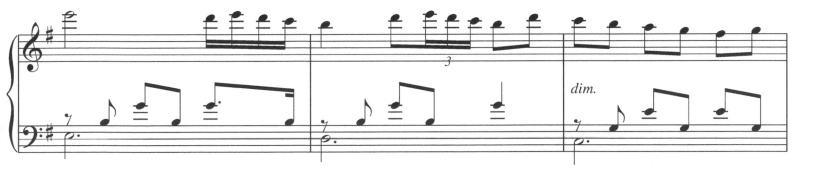

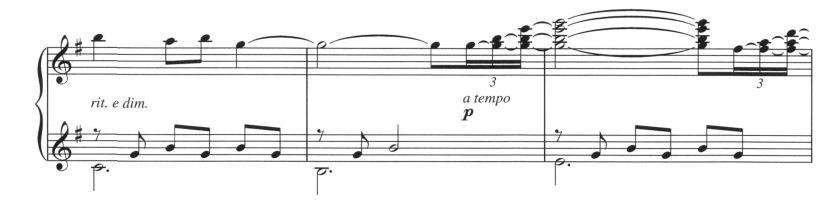

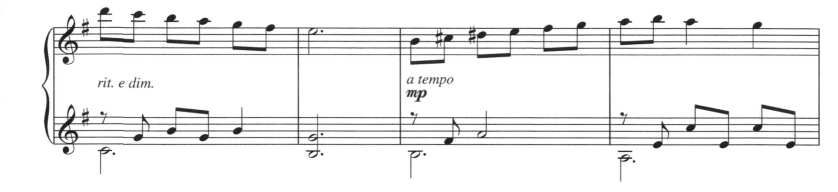

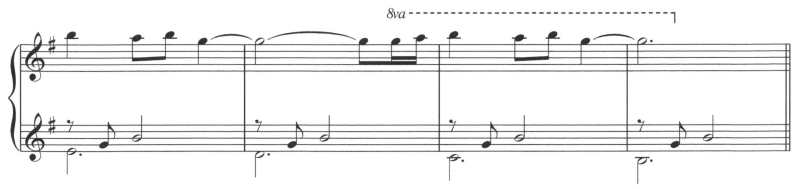

Slowly & freely

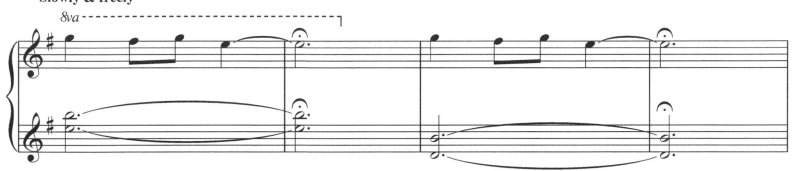

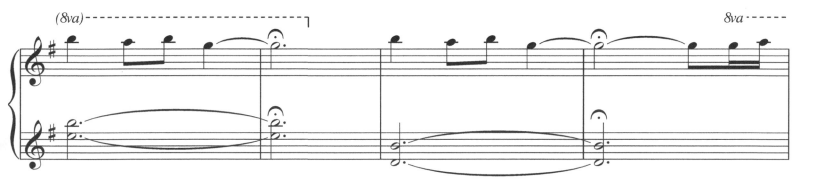

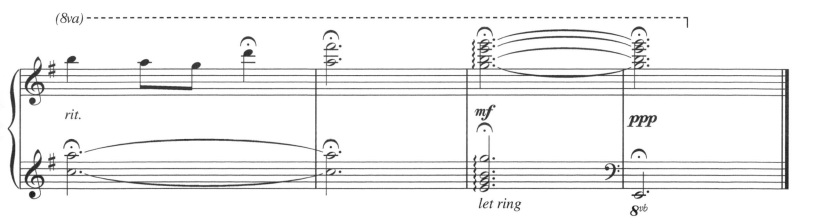

WE THREE KINGS

Traditional
Arranged by DAVID LANZ

Moderately slow, in 1

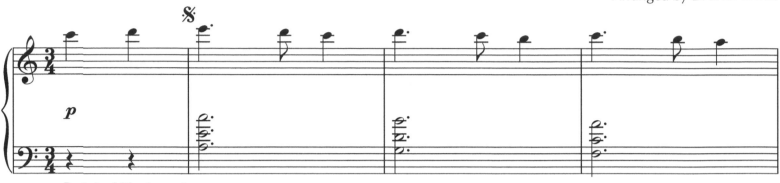

Pedal ad lib. throughout

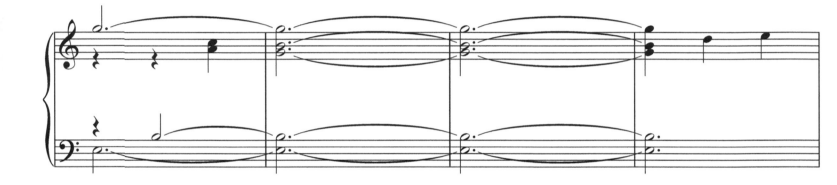

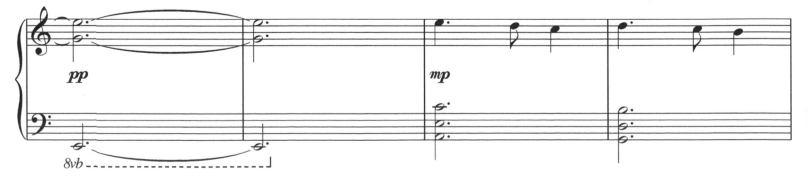

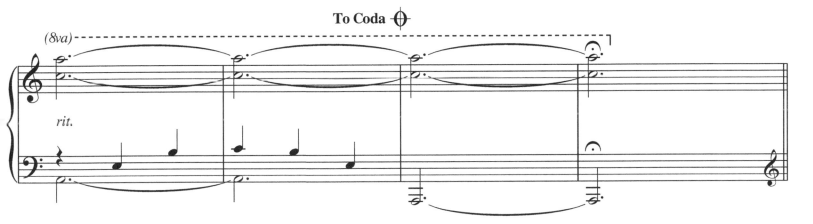

To Coda ⊕

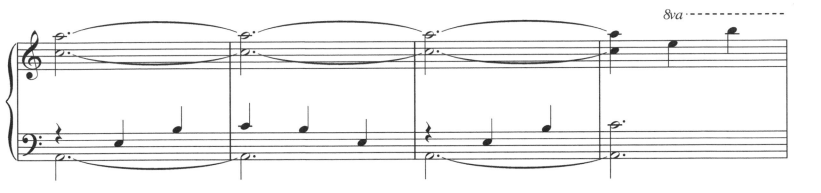

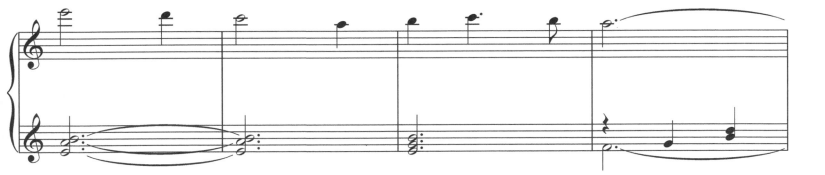

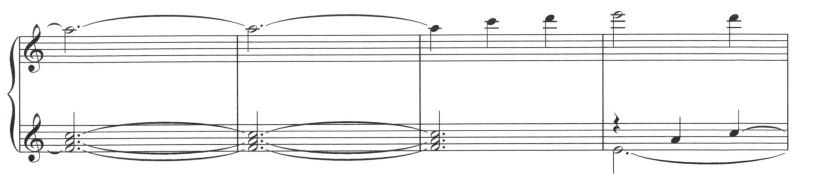

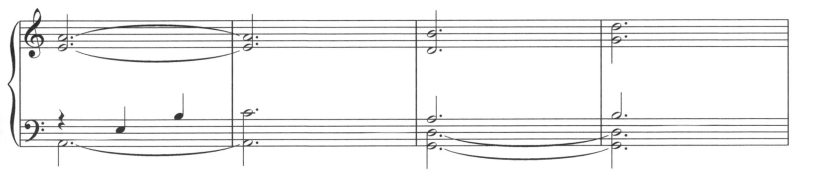

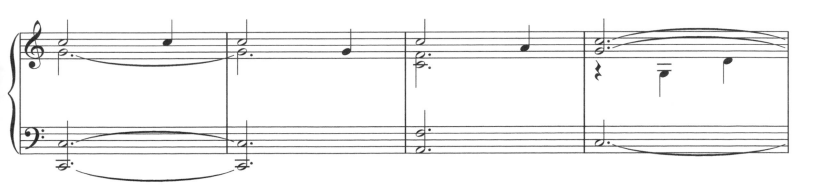

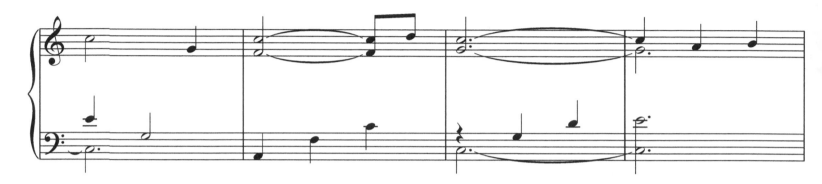

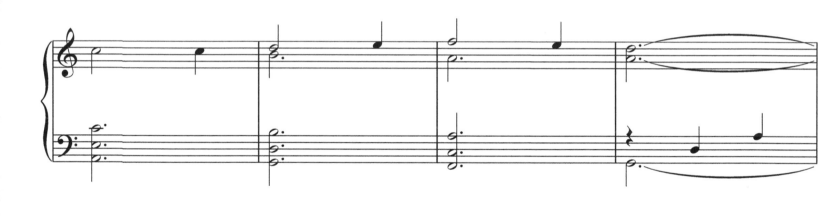

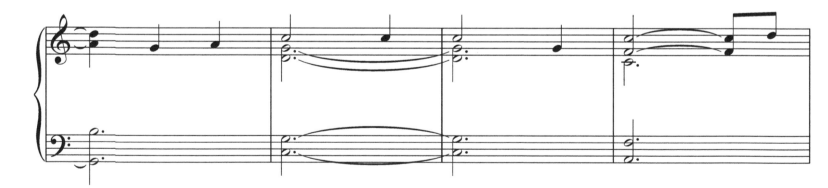

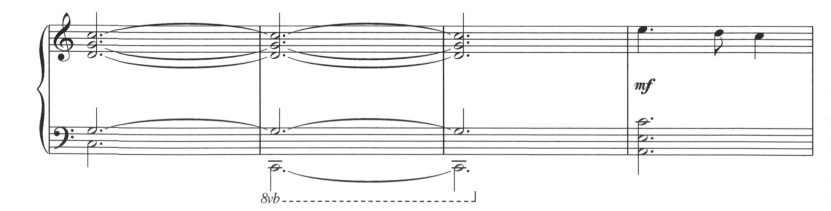

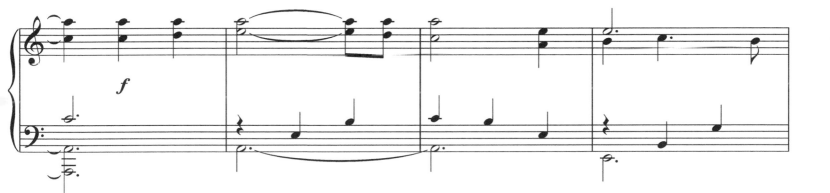

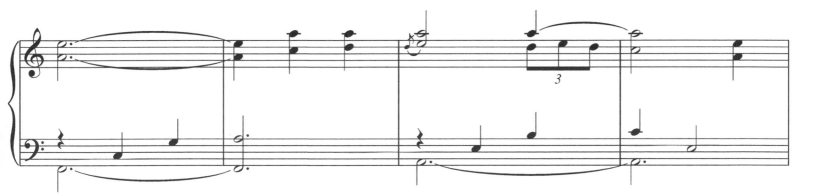

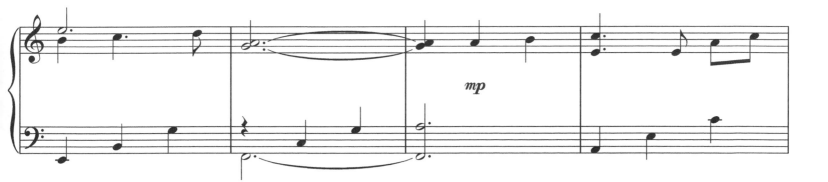

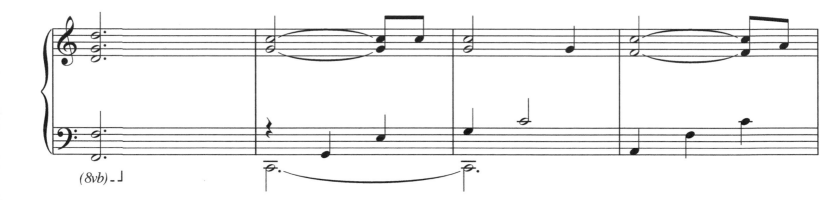

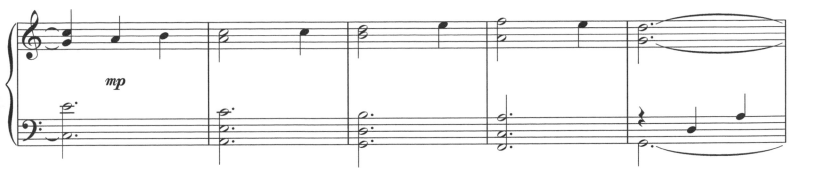

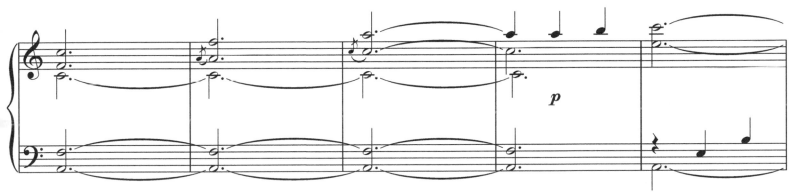

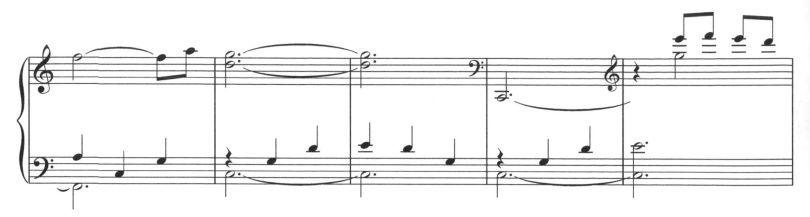

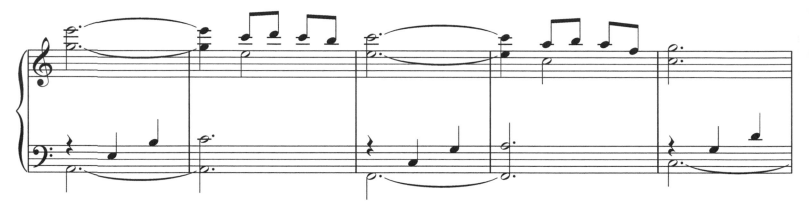

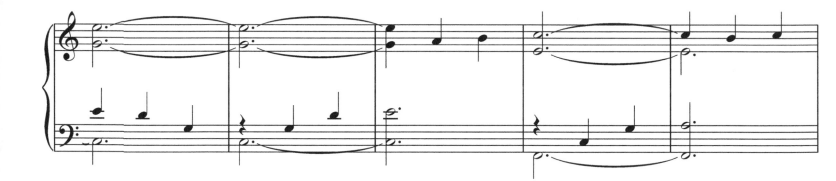

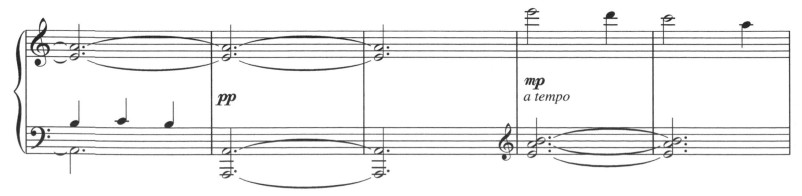

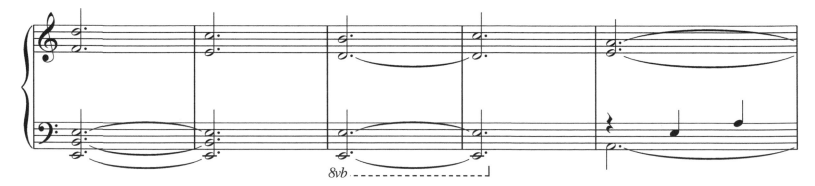

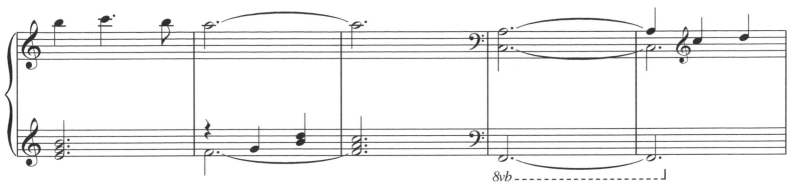

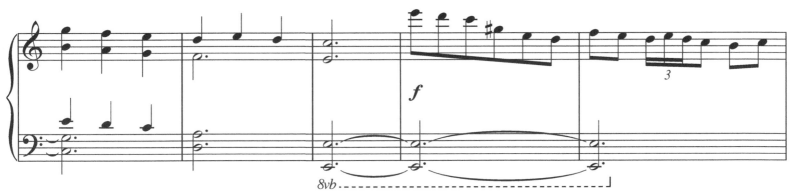

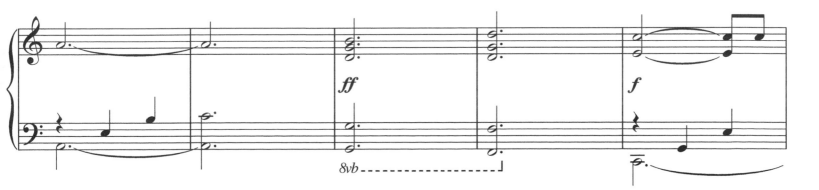

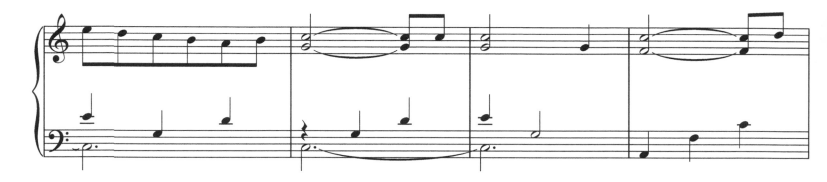

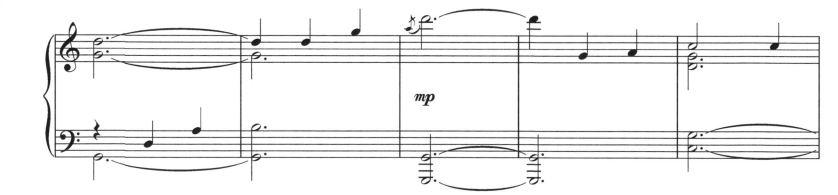

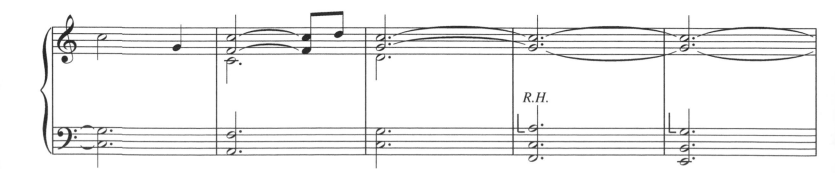

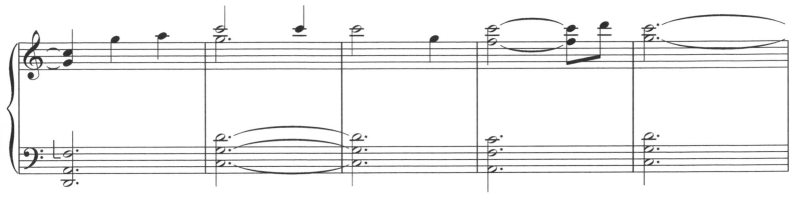

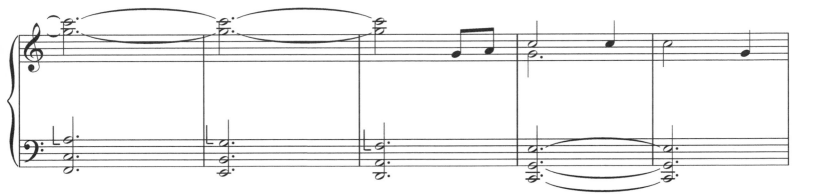

D.S. al Coda

CODA

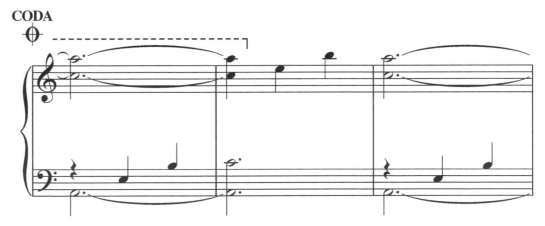

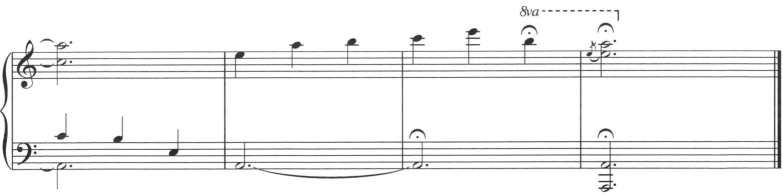

ANGEL DE LA NOCHE

By DAVID LANZ

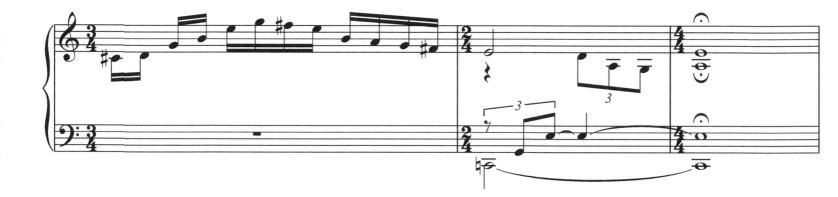

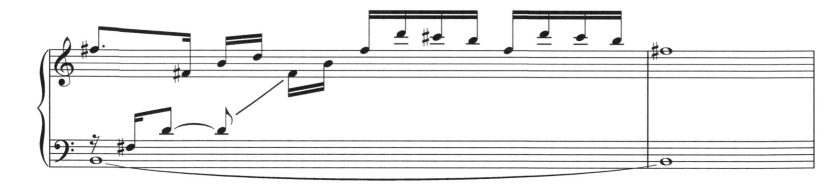

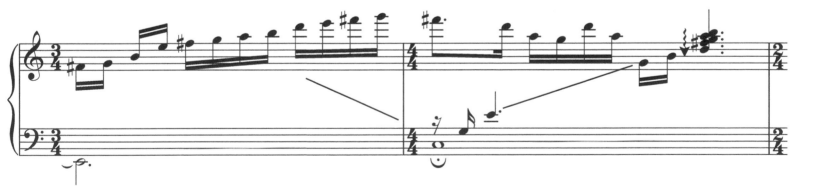

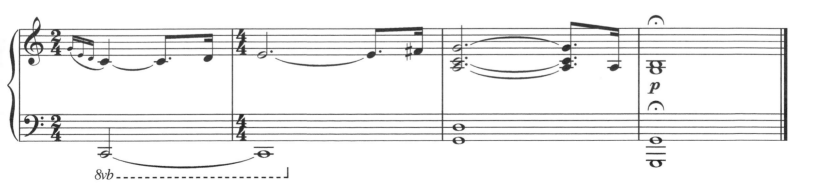

THE HOLLY & THE IVY

Traditional
Arranged by DAVID LANZ

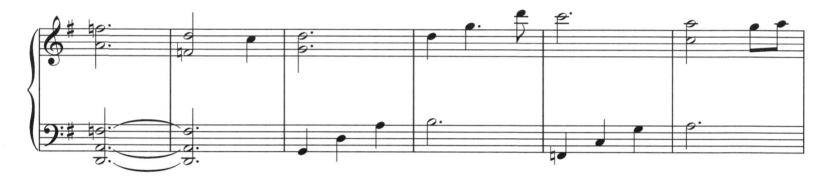

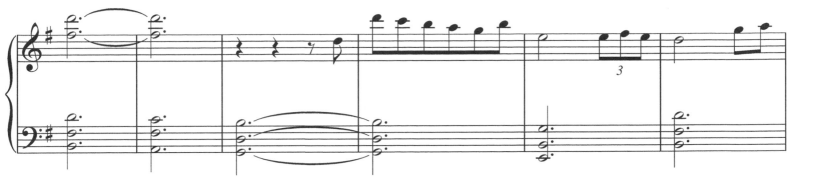

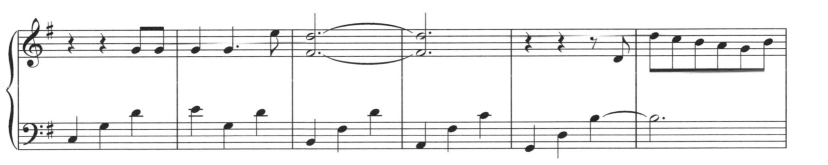

Ped.   ✻ Ped.   ✻ sim.

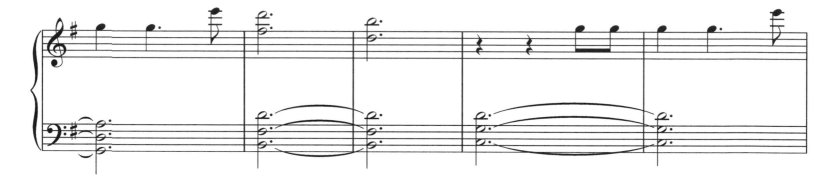

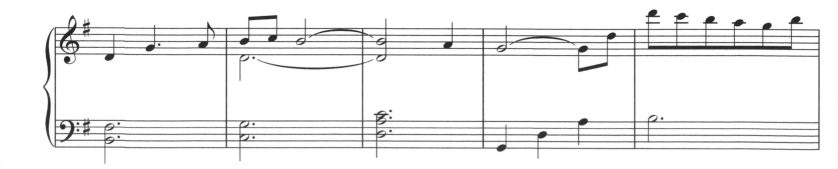

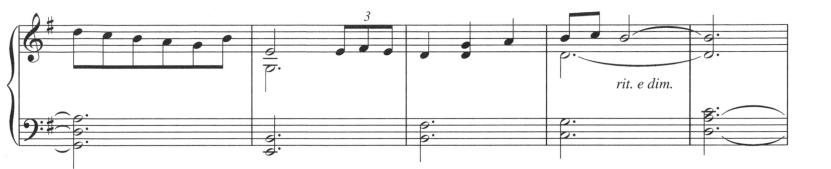

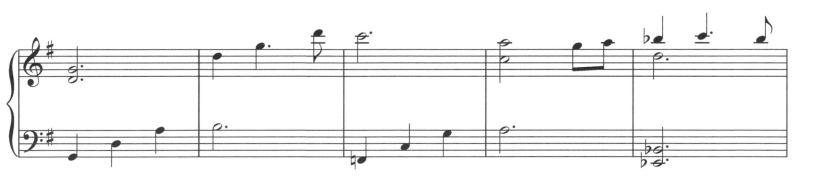

A DISTANT CHOIR

By DAVID LANZ

Very slowly and freely

With pedal

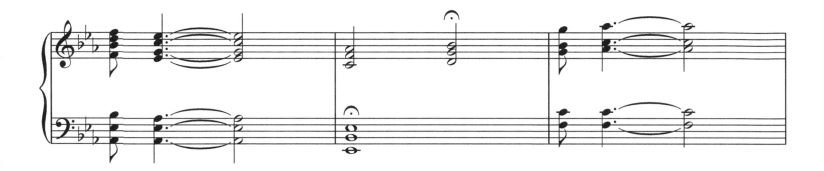

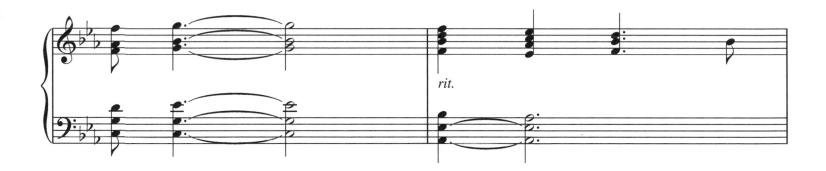

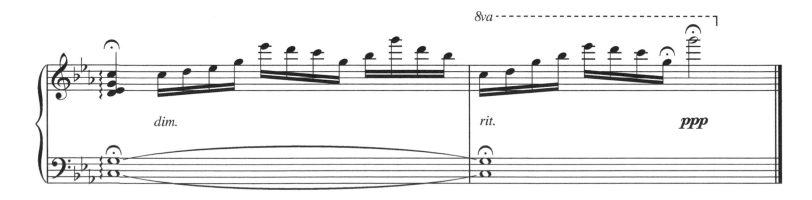